Collins

INTERNATIONAL PRIMARY ENGLISH

AS A SECOND LANGUAGE

Student's Book 3

Contents

About this book

This magazine-style Student's Book provides a wide variety of resources for classroom use and general enjoyment which act as the main stimulus (or "input") for the *Collins Cambridge Primary English as a Second Language* course. The modern presentation has been carefully designed to get the learners interested and involved in the learning process and to provide stimuli for discussion. The main aim is to make language learning both engaging and enjoyable, and to get learners thinking about themselves and the exciting world they live in.

You will find stories, short articles, poems, picture-dictionary pages, puzzles, maps, simple graphs and photographs linked to the topics for the year. The rich and varied visual resources provide interest and encourage oral communication and deeper thought about the topics.

Learners are guided through the material by clear, simple instructions which tell them what to read and give prompts for what else to do.

You will notice that there are coloured bubbles with small symbols on many of the pages.

This tells you that there is something to **talk** about.

This tells you that there is something to **think** about.

There are many opportunities for learners to talk about the materials. Talking should be encouraged and learners should not be afraid to talk about what they can see and what they have read. Talking about their ideas allows them to use the language they are learning and improves their confidence and fluency. Sometimes they will need to use their mother tongue when sharing their ideas, experiences and deeper thoughts. This is a natural part of fluency development and should not be received negatively. Allow learners to express themselves fluently and confidently in the mother tongue, and then support them with the vocabulary they need to say it in English too!

Above all, learners should be enjoying their learning as this develops a positive and inquisitive approach to the world around them and their place within it.

The authors

Family and friends

Read about Lee Chan and his family. Talk about your family.

Hello! My name is Lee Chan. I would like to tell you about my family.

My father is a pilot and my mother is a teacher. My sister is older than I am. She is twelve years old. I am nine years old. My baby brother is six months old. He cries a lot when he is hungry!

This is a picture of my family. My sister's name is Sandy. My baby brother's name is Steven. My father's name is King Fai. My mother's name is Kelly.

Sandy and I like baking. I like eating chocolate cakes. My sister likes eating biscuits.

My grandmother and grandfather are visiting us. They love being in the garden. They like listening to the birds.

This is my baby brother, Steven. He is laughing. He likes playing with his toes.

My cousin and I like swimming. My cousin's name is Meg.

Here is a picture of me with my friends. We all go to the same school.

Families are all different. Talk about your family.

My neighbourhood

Talk about the picture. What can you see in your neighbourhood?

Talk about which of these places you have in your neighbourhood.

school

library

dentist

swimming pool

doctor's surgery

toy shop

supermarket

What places do you like to visit in your neighbourhood?

In the classroom

Look at the picture of some children who are working hard in class. Then read the poem about some children who are *not* working hard in class.

My School

My teacher turned her back
And Sameer took the gap
To throw a paper aeroplane –
Oh what a naughty chap!

Mariam laughed at Billy,
And Jerry bounced a ball
It landed next to Eli
And bounced against the wall.

Susie wrote a letter
And passed it onto Lin
But Harry found it on the floor
And put it in the bin.

Fadi snapped his ruler
It made an awful noise
My teacher turned around again
"Be quiet, girls and boys!"

Jennifer Martin

Talk about your classroom. Is it like the classroom in the picture, or is it like the classroom in the poem?

Celebrations

Read about four different celebrations around the world.

Children in China

Chinese New Year is the longest and most important celebration in the Chinese calendar. People wear red clothes. Children are given 'lucky money' in red envelopes and families eat delicious meals. Many people set off fireworks as well. Chinese New Year ends with a beautiful lantern festival. The highlight of the lantern festival is the dragon dance. Some dancing dragons are 100 m long! They are made of silk, paper and bamboo.

Children in Thailand

Loy Krathong is Thailand's festival of lights. It takes place at the end of each year during a full moon. Families make a krathong. This is a small floating object filled with flowers and a candle. Some people add charms for good luck. When it is dark, people gather next to water and release their floats. If your krathong floats away from you, it means you will have good luck for the next year.

Children in Turkey

April 23 is 'Çocuk Bayrami' or Children's Day in Turkey. Children all over Turkey dress up in the national costume. Boys wear baggy silk trousers, a colourful vest top, a white shirt and a special hat called a tepelik. Girls wear a long colourful gown called a kaftan. Many children act in plays or musicals. The highlight of Çocuk Bayrami takes place in Turkey's capital, Ankara, where children from all over the world sing and dance in a colourful parade.

What is your favourite special day in your country? Talk about the celebrations.

Children in India

People in India celebrate a different festival of lights during Diwali each year. Diwali lasts for five days. Families decorate their homes with flowers and place small oil lamps called diyas, candles and coloured electric lights all around their houses. They also draw colourful rangoli, a pattern made in rice flour, at the front door.

Party pictures

Look at the party pictures.
Talk about what you
can see.

What food
do you like
to eat at a
party?

Which of these party ideas do you like?

Think of a party idea you would like. Tell your group about it.

Party snacks

It is important to follow recipes carefully. Read how to make these bright and colourful rainbow kebabs.

What you need:

- wooden skewers
- any type of washed fruit, such as apples, kiwis, grapefruit, strawberries, oranges, grapes, bananas and raspberries
- a small, sharp knife
- a small bowl

For the sauce:

- yoghurt and honey

What you do:

1. Choose your fruit.
2. Rinse the fruit that will not be peeled.
3. Peel or remove the skin if you need to.
4. Cut the large fruit into bite-sized chunks.
5. If you have chosen oranges or grapefruit, separate the segments.
6. Small fruits, like strawberries, raspberries and grapes don't need to be cut.
7. Push the fruit chunks carefully onto the wooden skewers, in any order you like.
8. Then mix some yoghurt and honey in a little bowl … dip, and eat!

What fruit would you use to make kebabs?

Baby elephants

Read how the elephant centre cares for the baby elephants.

What happens to baby animals if their parents cannot look after them? Some orphaned elephants get looked after in an elephant rescue centre.

A baby elephant is called a calf. When a calf is born, it's nearly one metre tall! Elephant calves drink ten litres of milk a day for the first year of their lives.

In the elephant centre, each calf is looked after by a few different keepers. It is important that the calves get used to different people. If an elephant becomes especially attached to one keeper, and that keeper leaves the rescue centre, the elephants get really sad and sick.

These baby elephants are drinking some milk.

Elephants are very clever and need to be kept occupied to stop them from becoming bored. The keepers take the baby elephants on long walks every day and also let them play with toys, like soccer balls!

When calves are two years old, the keepers move them to a national park to join older orphan elephants. Here they can live safely in the wild. During the day, calves mix with these wild elephants. They learn to use their trunks to get and eat plants.

The calves only spend time with the wild orphans during the day. At night they get looked after by keepers.

Elephants are very special animals. They never forget! Sometimes, when they are older, they come back to the rescue centre for help if they're hungry or hurt. Some elephants have even come to show keepers when they have a calf of their own! How do you think the keepers feel when this happens?

What happens if no one looks after animal orphans? Do you think it is important to help animal orphans?

Dreaming of dolphins

How much do you know about dolphins? Look at the photographs and read the information about swimming with dolphins.

Did you know that in some parts of the world you can swim in the ocean with wild dolphins? To do this, you need special equipment. You need to wear a wetsuit, a mask and snorkel, and fins. The equipment helps you stay safe and lets you breathe when your face is under the water.

Dolphins are exciting animals to watch. They dive up out of the water, and roll from side to side.

snorkel mask

wetsuit fins

Dolphins can swim very fast and like to leap out of the water.

They have a special kind of language for speaking to each other. They make clicking and squeaking noises!

They look very cute, and are often friendly and curious when they meet humans, but dolphins are wild animals. People need to respect the animals and their environment.

Would you like to swim with dolphins? Why? / Why not?

Important facts about dolphins

Dolphins live all over the world in seas and oceans. Some dolphins even live in rivers.

Dolphins eat fish, shrimps, squid and octopus. They hunt in groups.

Dolphins can swim up to 40 km per hour.

Dolphins call each other with clicking sounds.

A male dolphin can live up to 30 years. A female dolphin can live up to 50 years.

Dolphins need to be protected.

We must look after our sea. We must not throw litter and plastic into rivers and the oceans.

We must also stop overfishing.

What will happen if we don't look after dolphins?

Brown Bear and Wilbur Wolf

Listen and follow the story about Brown Bear and Wilbur Wolf.

Could a wolf and a bear be friends? What other animals might become friends? Why?

The world of birds

Read the text about birds.

You can see birds all around you. Look for them flying around in parks and gardens and at the beach.

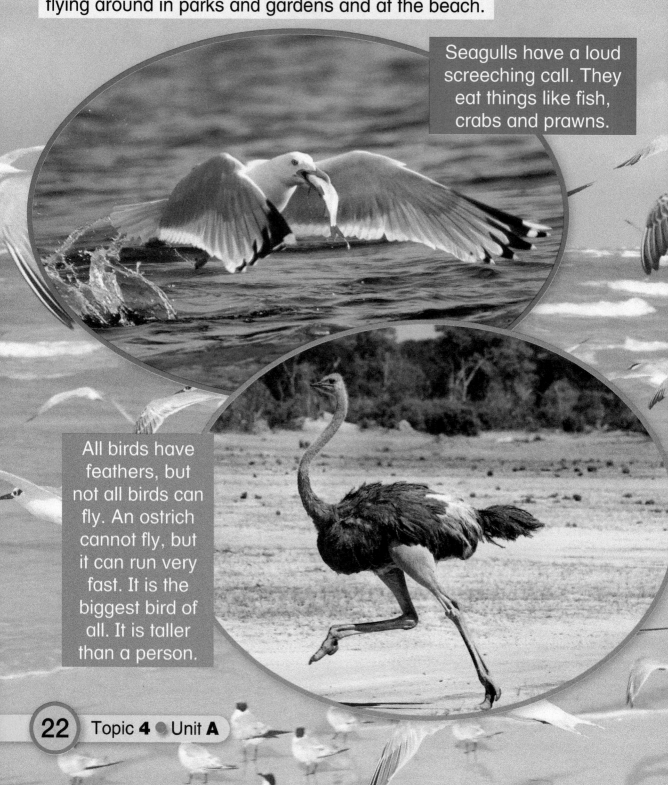

Seagulls have a loud screeching call. They eat things like fish, crabs and prawns.

All birds have feathers, but not all birds can fly. An ostrich cannot fly, but it can run very fast. It is the biggest bird of all. It is taller than a person.

Woodpeckers tap their beaks on tree trunks and make a loud rat-a-tat sound. They are looking for insects to eat.

Owls hunt at night. They can see in the dark and have strong beaks and sharp claws. Owls do not make any noise when they fly.

Do you know any birds that live in very cold or very hot places?

Parrots come from the Amazon rainforest. Some are red, yellow, blue or green. Some people keep parrots as pets. You can teach them to talk!

Could you do this?

Look at the photographs. Read the information and think about the questions.

We fly up to a height of 4,750 metres then we open the door to jump. You will feel a rush of cold air when we open the door and during the first part of your jump. Most people are so excited they don't notice the cold at all.

Could you jump out of an aeroplane?

You will free-fall for about 60 seconds before you open your parachute. But don't worry – you won't feel like you are falling at all. Free-falling is more like floating on a fluffy bed of air – you have to skydive to experience it!

Could you free-fall?

Some skydivers hold onto each other as they free-fall. They use a special grip to hold hands. This type of skydiving is also called bellyflying. Groups of four, eight and sixteen skydivers often take part in special competitions. The teams get points for style and how well they stay together as they free-fall.

Could you hold hands in the sky?

When you open your parachute you slow down quite quickly. You have to steer the parachute to make sure you land safely. Then you lift up your feet and slide to a stop. Someone on the ground will help you unhook the parachute.

Could you land like this?

Which do you think is more dangerous: swimming with dolphins or skydiving? Why?

Fly facts

You must have seen flies before, but how much do you really know about them?

Look at these pages from a website. Read the information about flies.

http://www.aflyfactswebsite.com

| FIND OUT ABOUT FLIES | HOUSEFLIES | FLY FACTS |

FLIES

Did you know? Most flying insects have four wings. Flies only have two, but they are fantastic flyers. They can fly up and down, sideways and even backwards. They can also hover and spin – you'll know this if you've ever tried to catch a fly!

HOUSEFLIES

There are more than 120,000 types of flies. The dark grey flies found around where we live are called houseflies. (The green and blue flies are called bottle flies.) Adult houseflies grow to a length of 7–10 millimetres. They only live for 15 to 25 days.

Colour: Dark grey to black

Shape: Oval

Length: 5–7 mm

Legs: 6

Wings: 2 only

Female flies lay 500–600 eggs in their short lives. Baby flies are called maggots – they look like little fat white worms. The maggots will change into flies after about two weeks.

DID YOU KNOW?
Doctors can use maggots to help people with serious wounds and burns. They put the maggots onto the wound and they eat all the damaged flesh. This helps the wound heal. Maggots don't eat healthy flesh at all.

FLY FACTS
Where do flies live?

Flies live all over the world. They are found in hot and cold places.

HOW DO FLIES EAT?

First of all, flies taste food with their feet! When they land on food, they know immediately if it's going to taste good or not. Their feet are 10 million times more sensitive to sweet tastes than your tongue.

Flies don't have teeth so they can't bite or chew. Their tongues work like sponges to soak up liquids. When a fly lands on solid food it spits or vomits onto the food to make it into a liquid that it can soak up. Flies love any wet and rotten food, especially things with a strong smell.

DO FLIES SPREAD GERMS?

One fly can carry over a million different kinds of germs. That's a lot of germs! Flies have hairs on their legs and sticky pads on their feet. Germs and small pieces of things the fly lands on get stuck to the hairs and pads. Flies rub their legs together to clean them and the small pieces fall off – sometimes onto your food or your skin! Germs on their feet spread when they walk on different surfaces.

ARE FLIES HELPFUL?

You already know that maggots can be used to help clean wounds. Flies also provide food for many other animals including spiders, frogs, fish and chameleons. They also help to recycle natural waste such as dead animals and dung. So, although flies are a pest and they spread germs, they also have their uses.

Too Hot to Stop

Listen to the story of Hoppitt the Gazelle and his friends.

In the desert in the east where the sand is so hot,

Hoppitt the Gazelle likes to hop, hop, hop!

Come and meet his friends in the desert sun.

Hop along with Hoppitt, the day has just begun!

The sand cat sat by the cactus tree.

"Come on, sand cat, come with me!"

The camel is a mammal with a hump upon his back.

"Follow us!" said the sand cat. "Follow our track."

"What's the hurry, Hoppitt?" asked the lizard in the shade.

"Come along, little lizard, join our parade."

"Won't you stop it, Hoppitt?" said the fox on the rocks.

"It's too hot to stop," said Hoppitt to the fox.

"Too hot to stop!" said the camel and the cat.

"Too hot to stop!" said the lizard at the back.

"Sss-stop it, Hoppitt, sss-stop it," hissed the snake on a dune.
"If you're hopping up there, you'd better stop soon."
"Stop it, Hoppitt, stop it," warned the falcon, flying by.
"I can see where you're heading, from high up in the sky."
Hoppitt hopped up the sand dune, so tall and so wide.
When he got to the top, he hopped off the other side …
SPLASH!
A lake full of water, so deep and so cool,
Hoppitt splashed down into the desert pool.
SPLOOSH! came the camel, the lizard, snake and cat,
The falcon and the fox, with a SPLISH, SPLOSH, SPLAT!
"At last …" said Hoppitt.
"This is where we stop it."

Can you think of any other animals that live in deserts?

Rally Challenge

Have you ever heard of rally car racing?
Read this article about a rally car race.

Rallying is a type of motorsport. A rally is a car race that takes place on public and private roads.

The Dunlop Targa Rally takes place in New Zealand over six days. The cars all start the race at different times, and the car that finishes each stage in the shortest time is the stage winner. The car that is fastest overall wins the rally.

Auckland

The Dunlop Targa Rally of New Zealand

This is the route for the rally.

New Plymouth

Hastings

Palmerston North

Wellington

— touring stage
— special stage

A rally is driven in stages. Each stage is a small race that is part of the main race. There are special stages and touring stages.

A special stage is a stage that is driven on roads that are closed to all other drivers. The rally drivers speed up on these stages because they don't have to worry about crashing into other cars.

To get from one special stage to another, the rally drivers use roads that are open to the public. These are called touring stages and the rally drivers have to obey all the rules of the road.

Should rallies be held in towns and cities? Why? / Why not?

The coldest place on Earth

Read about life in Antarctica. As you read, think about how hard it must be for the animals who live there.

Antarctica is the coldest and the windiest place on Earth. Temperatures can drop to –89°C (–129°F). The ocean around Antarctica has larger waves and stronger winds than anywhere else on Earth. In winter it gets so cold that even the snow freezes. Trees and bushes cannot grow there.

Some scientists live in special camps in Antarctica, but there are no towns or cities.

However, Antarctica is home to many animals, including orcas, seals and penguins. Seals are the penguins' greatest enemy.

Penguins are well suited to life in Antarctica. They have waterproof feathers and a thick layer of fat beneath their skin to keep them warm. This fat layer is called blubber.

Penguins cannot fly but they can swim very well. Penguins have to be great swimmers and divers because they get all of their food from the sea. Their wings are used to help them swim. King penguins feed on squid and fish. The smaller types of penguins feed mainly on krill, which are tiny creatures like shrimps.

King penguins only lay one egg, and look after it by balancing it on top of their feet. They do not build nests. A special pouch covers the egg and keeps it warm. The newborn chick lives safely inside the pouch. The chick is covered in a thick coat of brown, fluffy feathers. The mother and father penguins take turns to look after the eggs and chicks.

Can you think of other animals that live in very cold places?

Moving around the Sun

Read about the planets in our Solar System.

Venus is the brightest planet that can be seen from Earth. Venus has an atmosphere of sulfuric acid. Winds on Venus are very strong and fast.

Our home, planet Earth, is a very beautiful place. From a distance, our planet looks like a big blue marble. Earth is the only planet that humans, animals and plants can live on. Many people believe it is the only place in our Solar System where there is any life.

Mars

Earth is one of the planets that moves around (orbits) our Sun. The Sun and the planets are called the Solar System.

Earth

Mercury

Mars is also called the 'Red Planet' because it looks red when you view it through a telescope.

Venus

Mercury is the closest planet to the Sun. It has no atmosphere so there is no wind or rain there. The surface of Mercury is full of big holes called craters.

Saturn is surrounded by seven rings made of tiny pieces of rock and ice. You can see these rings from Earth through a telescope.

Neptune was visited by the spacecraft Voyager 2 on August 25, 1989.

Pluto

Neptune

Uranus

Saturn

Pluto is furthest from the Sun. It is so small it is called a 'dwarf planet'. Pluto is a dark and frozen place.

Jupiter

Uranus is four times the size of Earth. It looks blue-green through a telescope. There are also very strong winds blowing on Uranus.

Jupiter is the largest planet in our Solar System. Jupiter is a very stormy planet. The Great Red Spot on Jupiter is a massive storm that has gone on for over 300 years.

The word *solar* means having to do with the Sun. What do you think these things are? A solar-powered calculator, a solar water heater and a solar eclipse.

Let's Go to Mars!

Imagine travelling through the Solar System to Mars. What an exciting adventure! Read about things to do on Mars.

Are you ready for the trip of a lifetime?

Our spaceship

You will travel in comfort and safety in the latest spaceship. Don't worry about space junk hitting the spaceship because our spaceship has an extra-light, extra-strong skin that can repair itself if space junk hits it.

It takes five months to reach Mars, but if you book a ticket for the super-fast *Mars Express*, you will get to Mars in just three months!

In-flight entertainment

Enjoy the in-flight entertainment, including:

floating toothpaste

breakfast in a bottle

weightless football

What to wear

Be cool on Mars!

Our spacesuits have a stretchy undersuit with zip front and water-cooling tubes to keep you at the right temperature. There is even a drink bag inside the suit!

A **helmet** with **headphones** and **microphones** so you can talk to your family on Earth.

A stretchy undersuit with zip front and water-cooling tubes to keep you at the right temperature.

An in-suit drink bag.

Note: If you want to phone home, you'll have to wait almost 25 minutes for the person back on Earth to hear you. So phone conversations can take a long time!

What would you tell your friends if you phoned them from Mars?

What can you do on Mars?

Read about what you can do on Mars. Would you like to do any of these activities?

Build sandcastles.

Enter the dune buggy races.

Set a land speed record in a sand yacht.

Be blown about in gigantic sandstorms.

Hunt for signs of water.

5

Watch red sunsets in a pink sky. The Sun will look half as big as it does from Earth.

6

Look for signs of life.

7

Life on Mars

Have your photo taken under our sign.

8

Which activity on Mars would you do first? Why?

Space walk

If you look up at the night sky you can see the Moon. Can you imagine walking on the Moon? Read this newspaper article about the first person to walk on the Moon.

The Daily Times

LATE EDITION   MONDAY JULY 22, 1969

MAN MAKES IT TO THE MOON

Yesterday the astronaut Neil Armstrong stepped onto the Moon. He collected rock samples and planted the American flag before returning to his spaceship.

As he stepped onto the Moon, Neil Armstrong said, "That's one small step for man, one giant leap for mankind."

This footprint was made by one of the first astronauts to walk on the dusty surface of the Moon.

Imagine you were a reporter meeting the astronauts when they got back from the Moon. What questions would you ask them?

Space talk

Read about Galileo Galilei.

Galileo Galilei was born in Italy in 1564. He was an Italian scientist who studied the stars. At this time, people believed that the Earth was the most important part of the Solar System. They thought the Sun moved around the Earth.

Galileo did not agree – he believed that the planets moved around the Sun.

In 1609, Galileo invented the first telescope. A year later, he discovered that Jupiter had four moons, but nobody believed him.

In 1616, Galileo was told he was not allowed to teach the idea that the Sun is at the centre of the Solar System anymore. Galileo was put under house arrest and was not allowed to share his ideas.

Today we know he was right after all.

How do you feel when no one believes what you say?

Hector and the Cello

Read this story about Hector, a very determined hippo.

Hector the hippo wanted to play the cello more than anything else in the world.

But who in the wild, wet jungle would teach him?

Hector tramped through the jungle to find a cello teacher. First he met a lion. "I want to play the cello," said Hector. "Whoever heard of a hippo playing the cello?" roared the lion. He roared so loudly that his mane fell off. Hector picked up the lion's mane and draped it round his neck. It was going to be a chilly night in the wild, wet jungle.

On he tramped until … he met a leopard. "I want to play the cello," said Hector.

"Whoever heard of a hippo playing the cello?" growled the leopard. She growled so loudly that all her spots flew off. Hector picked up the spots and stuck them on his back. He might need a disguise in the wild, wet jungle.

On he tramped until … he met a rhino. "I want to play the cello," said Hector.

"Whoever heard of a hippo playing the cello?" snorted the rhino. He snorted so loudly that his horn fell off. Hector picked up the horn and went on his way. He could blow on the horn if he got lost.

How do you think the story is going to end? Share your ideas.

On he tramped until … he met a slithery snake. "I want to play the cello," said Hector.

"SSSSSSSSSS. Hisssssssssss. SSSSTUPID! SSSSSILLY! SSSSAD!" hissed the snake. She hissed so much that she slithered out of her skin. Hector picked up the skin. He might need a cloth to wipe his cello in the wild, wet jungle.

On and on he tramped until ... he met a lyrebird. "I want to play the cello," said Hector. "Please don't roar, or growl, or snort, or hiss."

"Do you have a cello?" asked the lyrebird.

"No," said Hector. "But I have a lion's mane, a leopard's spots, a rhino's horn and a snake's skin. Will that buy me a cello and some lessons?"

"Of course!" said the lyrebird, who was a good musician.

Every single day for two years, Hector tramped happily through the wild, wet jungle for his cello lessons.

Two years and one day later, there was a grand concert. All the animals from the jungle came.

Hector started to play. The sound was so sweet …

The lion roared for more.

The leopard growled with glee.
The rhino snorted with surprise.
The snake hissed with happiness.
So the musician gave the lion his mane back.
He gave the leopard her spots back.
… and the snake her skin.
He gave the rhino his horn …
In the wild, wet jungle the animals made music
until midnight.

What message
does this story
give?

The Brave Baby

Look at the pictures. They tell a story about a Chief and a baby who was not scared of him.

There was once a brave and fierce Chief. The people in the village were scared of him.

"Wasso, a little baby, is not scared of you," said a wise woman. "Look – she is playing with a stick."

The Chief wanted Wasso to tell him why she was not afraid of him. Wasso began to cry. She would not go to the chief!

Why do you think baby Wasso wasn't scared of the Chief?

4

The Chief tried to make Wasso stop crying. He danced a special dance.

5

Wasso liked the special dance – it made her happy, so she stopped crying. She soon fell asleep.

6

"You are right, Wise Woman, Wasso is not scared of me!" exclaimed the Chief. He was so tired from dancing that he also fell asleep!

Hansel and Gretel

A play script is written with parts for each character in a play. This play has parts for seven characters. Work in groups of seven. Read the play aloud.

NARRATOR: Hansel and Gretel lived with their father and stepmother on the edge of a large forest. Their father, who was a very kind man, was worried. One day, he said to his wife (who was a very cruel woman) …

WOODCUTTER: What can we do? I need to feed my children, but I can't earn enough money.

STEPMOTHER: Well, you will have to do something. Why don't you send them away?

NARRATOR: The woodcutter and his wife argued all night. The next morning, the woodcutter walked slowly to where his children were sitting.

WOODCUTTER: Hansel, Gretel, come with me. We are going for a walk in the forest.

GRETEL: That will be fun. We will have a picnic there.

NARRATOR: Now Hansel, who had heard his parents arguing all night long, knew that they were not going to have a picnic. He was a very smart boy, and he hid a bread roll in his jacket pocket. Gretel chatted merrily to her father and Hansel walked behind them, throwing down crumbs along the way.

WOODCUTTER: Let's stop here, children. Run along and play for a little while. I shall sit here and wait for you. You will have lots of fun playing in the forest.

NARRATOR: When Hansel and Gretel returned, their father was gone.

GRETEL: Oh no! What will happen to us? It is getting dark and I am scared.

HANSEL: Don't be scared, Gretel. I dropped some crumbs on the path. We will look for them and they will guide us home.

NARRATOR: Unfortunately, the birds had seen the crumbs and had eaten them up. Hansel who was a brave and a smart boy decided to find his own way home, but it became too dark to see, and the children were soon lost.

GRETEL: Hansel, I'm hungry and tired. Please let me rest for a little while.

NARRATOR:	Just then, the children saw lights twinkling in the distance. They ran quickly towards them, to see the most beautiful little cottage. The roof and the walls were decorated with sweets and biscuits and the curtains looked like candy floss! Hansel knocked carefully on the door.
OLD WOMAN:	Who is knocking at my door? One knock, two knocks, three knocks, four.
HANSEL:	Good evening, ma'am. Could you help us? My sister and I are lost.
OLD WOMAN:	Lost? Lost? That can't be true. Your family will look for you.
NARRATOR:	Hansel and Gretel were too tired to explain what had happened to them. The old woman invited them in.
OLD WOMAN:	Hahaha hee hee hee. Lovely children, just for me! I shall eat them, one by one, Yummy food inside my tum!
NARRATOR:	Hansel heard the old woman talking to herself. He whispered to Gretel…
HANSEL:	Gretel, that old lady is wicked. We must escape from here. We must run faster than the wind!
NARRATOR:	The old woman who was also a bit deaf was so busy stirring a stew in her cauldron that she did not hear the children creep carefully out of the house. They ran like the wind until they could no longer see the lights twinkling in the night sky. Hansel and Gretel were too tired to walk anymore and they fell asleep on

the soft, soft grass under a tree. The next morning, when they awoke, they thought they were dreaming, for there, sitting watch over them, was an owl.

OWL: Don't be scared. I will help you get back home safely. Just follow me.

NARRATOR: The children happily followed the owl, and before they knew it, they were back home again.

WOODCUTTER: Oh my children, I am so happy to see you! I have been looking all over for you! Come inside at once!

NARRATOR: The woodcutter had changed his mind about leaving his children in the forest, but when he reached the place where he had first left Hansel and Gretel, they were nowhere to be seen. He had spent the whole night looking anxiously for them. The stepmother was so surprised and angry to see Hansel and Gretel that she stormed off into the forest, never to be seen again. As for the woodcutter and his children, they lived happily ever after.

What fairy tales do you know from your country?

Look, but don't touch!

Read about some dangerous but wonderful sea animals.

The sea can be dangerous for humans, but it is also dangerous for some of the animals that live beneath the waves. Just like land animals, sea animals protect themselves.

Look at this triggerfish. It has a sharp spine on its head. Ouch!

This sting ray stays safe because it is electric. If you touch it you will get an electric shock. So, don't touch!

The porcupine fish has spines, too. It fills with water when it feels threatened and looks like a big spiky ball. Would you want to play with it?

Eek! Did you know you get snakes in the sea? This sea snake has teeth called 'fangs'. Its bite is poisonous.

Jellyfish can sting you with their long, poisonous tentacles.

What other dangerous but wonderful sea animals do you know about?

Crocodiles and monitor lizards

Crocodiles and lizards have lived on Earth for millions of years. Look at the photographs and read about these animals.

Crocodiles

Large crocodiles only need a few big meals a year. The rest of the time they mostly eat fish.

Crocodiles are some of the best hunters in the world. They are good at sneaking up on their prey. Crocodiles grab their prey with their powerful jaws. They can snap their jaws shut with enough power to crush a car door.

Crocodiles catch their prey and try to drown it by pulling it underwater. Crocodiles have a flap of skin to stop water going down their throats, so they can go underwater with their mouths open.

Which animal do you think is more dangerous: a shark or a crocodile? Why?

Monitor lizards

Monitor lizards look a bit like crocodiles. Their mouths contain poison and even if their prey escapes, it will often die later from blood poisoning.

Monitor lizards are scavengers. They will eat anything they can find. They eat fish, dead animals, birds, frogs and other small animals.

Baby monitor lizards often live in trees where they are safe from adult lizards who even eat baby lizards.

But like crocodiles, once they become adults, they are clever predators.

What other predators can you think of?

Big, bigger, the biggest

The three biggest animals in Africa are called 'The Big Three'. Read the information to learn more about them.

The huge African savannah is made up of grassland and some woodland. It's home to three of the largest animals on Earth: elephants, rhinos and hippos.

Elephants are the biggest of The Big Three.

An adult elephant can weigh 6,300 kg. How much would three elephants weigh?

Hippos are smaller than elephants and live on the banks of rivers and lakes.

Rhinos are also smaller than elephants but they can be as big as trucks.

Poachers get a lot of money for elephant tusks and rhino horns. Think of ways to protect these animals from poachers.

The Big Three are all endangered animals. This means that we need to protect them to make sure they can survive in the future.

Humans are the worst enemies of elephants, rhinos and hippos.

People kill elephants for their ivory tusks. They kill hippos for meat and oil, and rhinos for their horns.

Game wardens try to stop the poachers, but many animals are still killed. We need to protect Africa's big three animals before they are all gone.

Marco Polo

Read about a famous adventurer called Marco Polo.

Many people have asked me to tell the story of my life, so here it is.

I was born in 1254 CE, in the city of Venice in Italy, but I only met my father when I was 15 years old. Imagine that! My father and uncle left on a trading trip to Asia before I was born. They only returned when I was 15 years old.

When I was 17, my father and uncle left on another trip, but this time they took me with them! I was so excited – all I wanted was to see new places and meet new people and learn about new things! We ended up staying away from home for more than 20 years!

It was such an exciting adventure that I hardly noticed the passing of time. I saw so many strange and wonderful things and met many interesting people. I learned to speak Chinese, and Kublai Khan, the ruler of China, was so impressed by me he made me his ambassador and sent me all around the country on business.

We finally returned to Venice in 1295 CE. Many people do not believe my stories, but that's fine with me.

Captain Scott

Read about a brave explorer called Robert Scott.

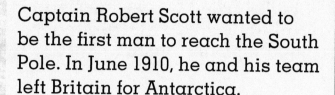

Captain Robert Scott wanted to be the first man to reach the South Pole. In June 1910, he and his team left Britain for Antarctica.

They reached the South Pole on 17 January, 1912, but they were shocked to find out that they were not the first to get there. Roald Amundsen, an explorer from Norway, and his team had got to the South Pole first!

Bravely, Scott and his men turned to go back to the base camp. They were very tired and cold and hungry, and to make matters worse, they ran out of food and fuel on their way back. Scott had been keeping a diary, and on 29 March, 1912, he wrote: "The end cannot be far. It seems a pity but I do not think I can write more."

Sadly, all the men died before they reached their base camp.

Eight months later, on 12 November, 1912, their tent was found. A monument was made with blocks of ice. Although they did not reach their goal, they were still heroes!

How would you have felt if you were Captain Scott?

Amelia Earhart

Imagine flying across the world in a tiny aeroplane! Amelia Earhart decided to fly around the world long before we had modern planes. Read about her adventures.

Amelia Earhart was born in 1897, in Kansas, USA. Amelia saw her first plane when she was ten, but she did not think much of it at all! She called the plane a thing of rusty nails and wood!

When she was nearly 40, Amelia decided that she was ready for a last, big challenge and wanted to be the first woman to fly around the world on her own.

Her first attempt was unsuccessful because her plane was damaged. Then, in June 1937, she and Fred Noonan, her navigator, decided to try again.

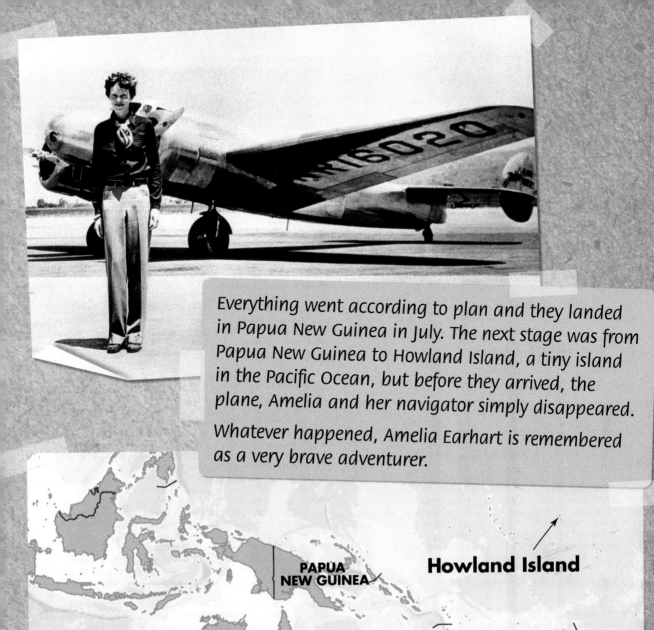

Everything went according to plan and they landed in Papua New Guinea in July. The next stage was from Papua New Guinea to Howland Island, a tiny island in the Pacific Ocean, but before they arrived, the plane, Amelia and her navigator simply disappeared.

Whatever happened, Amelia Earhart is remembered as a very brave adventurer.

Howland Island

PAPUA NEW GUINEA

AUSTRALIA

Can you think of any other famous people who disappeared?

An imprint of HarperCollins*Publishers*
The News Building
1 London Bridge Street
London SE1 9GF

HarperCollins*Publishers*
1st Floor, Watermarque Building, Ringsend Road
Dublin 4, Ireland

browse the complete Collins catalogue at
www.collins.co.uk

© HarperCollins*Publishers* Limited 2017

10 9 8 7 6 5 4 3

ISBN 978-0-00-821364-0

British Library Cataloguing in Publication Data
A catalogue record for this publication is available from the British Library.

Publisher Celia Wigley
Commissioning editor Karen Jamieson
Series editor Karen Morrison
Editor Alexander Rutherford
Project managed by Tara Alner
Edited by Cassandra Fox
Proofread by Zoe Smith
Cover design by ink-tank and associates
Cover artwork by QBS Learning
Internal design by Ken Vail Graphic Design
Typesetting by Ken Vail Graphic Design
Illustrations by QBS Learning
Production by Lauren Crisp

Printed and bound by CPI Group (UK) Ltd, Croydon CR0 4YY

Acknowledgements

The publishers gratefully acknowledge the permissions granted to reproduce copyright material in the book. Every effort has been made to contact the holders of copyright material, but If any have been inadvertently overlooked, the Publisher will be pleased to make the necessary arrangements at the first opportunity.

HarperCollins*Publishers* Limited for extracts and artwork from:

Brown Bear and Wilbur Wolf by Sarah Parry, illustrated by Judy Musselle, text © 2012 Sarah Parry. *Fly Facts* by Janice Marriott, illustrated by Andy Keylock, text © 2004 Janice Marriott. *Too Hot to Stop!* by Stephen Webb, illustrated by Stephen Webb, text © 2010 Stephen Webb. *Let's Go To Mars!* by Janice Marriott, illustrated by Mark Ruffle, text © 2005 Janice Marriott. *Hector and the Cello* by Ros Asquith, illustrated by Ros Asquith, text © 2005 Ros Asquith. *The Brave Baby* by Malachy Doyle, illustrated by Richard Johnson, text © 2004 Malachy Doyle. *Hansel and Gretel* by Malachy Doyle, illustrated by Tim Archbold, text © 2006 Malachy Doyle.

Photo acknowledgements

The publishers wish to thank the following for permission to reproduce photographs. Every effort has been made to trace copyright holders and to obtain their permission for the use of copyright materials. The publishers will gladly receive any information enabling them to rectify any error or omission at the first opportunity.

(t = top, c = centre, b = bottom, r = right, l = left)

Cover & p1 QBS Learning, p7 (background) Inga Linder/Shutterstock, p10t Cora Reed/Shutterstock, p10c testing/Shutterstock, p10b GOLFX/Shutterstock, p11t muratart/Shutterstock, p11c muratart/Shutterstock, p11b India Picture/Shutterstock, p12-13 gui jun peng/Shutterstock, p12t wavebreakmedia/Shutterstock, p12l Monkey Business Images/Shutterstock, p12b Robert Kneschke/Shutterstock, p12r EvgeniiAnd/Shutterstock, p13tl Sergey Novikov/Shutterstock, p13tr B Calkins/Shutterstock, p13bl eldirector77/Shutterstock, p13br Peter Baxter/Shutterstock, p14-15 paprika/Shutterstock, p14 Ozgur Coskun/Shutterstock, p15 iuliia_n/Shutterstock, p16-17 Jordi C/Shutterstock, p16t Barbara von Hoffmann/Alamy, p16bl Gary Roberts/REX/Shutterstock, p16br Gerry Ellis/ Minden Pictures/Getty, p17 Lisa Hoffner/naturepl, p18t Beth Swanson/Shutterstock, p18b Willyam Bradberry/Shutterstock, p19t Paul Vinten/Shutterstock, p19c Steven Ramzy/Shutterstock, p19b MOHAMED ABDULRAHEEM/Shutterstock, p22-23 Mark Winfrey/Shutterstock, p22t Juho Salo/Shutterstock, p22b paula french/Shutterstock, p23t Tobyphotos/Shutterstock, p23c duangnapa_b/Shutterstock, p23b Operation Shooting/Shutterstock, p24t Germanskydiver/Shutterstock, p24b Mauricio Graiki/Shutterstock, p25t Germanskydiver/Shutterstock, p25b Dreamframer/Shutterstock, p26t kurt_G/Shutterstock, p26b Latte Art/Shutterstock, p27 Cathy Keifer/Shutterstock, p28 (background) Andrea Willmore/Shutterstock, p30-31 Andy and Angie Belcher, p30t Andy and Angie Belcher, p31b Andy and Angie Belcher, p31t Andrea Willmore/Shutterstock, p32-33 Li Hui Chen/Shutterstock, p32 vladsilver/Shutterstock, p33 Roger Clark ARPS/Shutterstock, p34-35 Macrovector/Shutterstock, p36-37 (background) chonlathit_stock/Shutterstock, p38-39 (background esfera/Shutterstock, p40 (background) nienora/Shutterstock, p40bl neftali/Shutterstock, p40br Castleski/Shutterstock, p41tr iryna1/Shutterstock, p41bl Vadim Sadovski/Shutterstock, p50-51 (background) Nearbirds/Shutterstock, p52-53 (background) GraphicsRF/Shutterstock, p54tr Rich Carey/Shutterstock, p54bl stephan kerkhofs/Shutterstock, p55tl Jung Hsuan/Shutterstock, p55tr Beth Swanson/Shutterstock, p55br Rich Carey/Shutterstock, p55bl feathercollector/Shutterstock, p56-57 (background) komkrit Preechachanwate/Shutterstock, p56r Audrey Snider-Bell/Shutterstock, p56l Jonathan and Angela Scott, p57l E. O/Shutterstock, p57r Natali Glado/Shutterstock, p58-59 Galyna Andrushko/Shutterstock, p58b Donovan van Staden/Shutterstock, p59t Travel Stock/Shutterstock, p59c GUDKOV ANDREY/Shutterstock, p59b Svetlana Foote/Shutterstock, p60 (background) hvaygert Ekaterina/Shutterstock, p60t rook76/Shutterstock, p60b The Print Collector / Alamy Stock Photo, p61 (background) Igor Janicek/Shutterstock/Shutterstock, p61t Time Life Pictures/Mansell/Getty Images, p62t Everett Historical/Shutterstock, p62b Everett Historical/Shutterstock, p63t Everett Historical/Shutterstock, p63b © Collins Bartholomew Ltd 2017